Globalization Unveiled: Assessing the Impact of the World Trade Organization

ROBERTO MIGUEL RODRIGUEZ

Copyright Page

TITLE: Globalization Unveiled: Assessing the Impact of the World Trade Organization

1ST Edition

Table of Contents

Globalization Unveiled: Assessing the Impact of the World Trade Organization

By Roberto Miguel Rodriguez

Chapter 1: The World Trade Organization: History, Functions, Strengths, and Weaknesses

The Origins of the World Trade Organization

The World Trade Organization (WTO) is a global organization that deals with the rules of trade between nations. It was established on January 1, 1995, following the conclusion of the Uruguay Round of negotiations, which lasted from 1986 to 1994. However, the origins of the WTO can be traced back to several earlier initiatives.

The precursor to the WTO was the General Agreement on Tariffs and Trade (GATT), which was created in the aftermath of World War II. GATT aimed to reduce trade barriers and promote economic cooperation among nations. GATT successfully negotiated several rounds of trade liberalization, but it lacked a strong institutional framework and enforcement mechanism.

The need for a more comprehensive and effective international trade organization led to the establishment of the WTO. The Uruguay Round negotiations, which laid the groundwork for the WTO, addressed a wide range of trade issues, including tariffs, non-tariff barriers, intellectual property rights, and services. The negotiations also aimed to bring developing countries into the global trading system on more favorable terms.

The creation of the WTO was a significant milestone in the history of international trade. It represented a shift from ad hoc negotiations to a more institutionalized and rules-based system. The WTO's main functions include administering trade agreements, facilitating trade negotiations, and providing a forum for resolving trade disputes.

The WTO has faced criticism from various quarters. Developing countries often argue that the organization's rules and procedures favor developed nations, limiting their ability to protect their domestic industries and pursue their development objectives. Non-governmental organizations (NGOs) have also criticized the WTO for its lack of transparency and accountability.

Despite these criticisms, the WTO has played a crucial role in promoting global economic integration and stability. It has helped reduce trade barriers, increase market access, and provide a platform for resolving trade disputes. The organization has also contributed to the promotion of sustainable development, gender equality, and fair trade practices.

In conclusion, the World Trade Organization emerged from the ashes of World War II and the earlier GATT negotiations. It has since become a key player in shaping the rules of international trade. While it has faced its fair share of challenges, the WTO continues to play a vital role in fostering economic cooperation and promoting a more inclusive and sustainable global trading system.

The Evolution of the World Trade Organization

The World Trade Organization (WTO) has undergone significant evolution since its establishment in 1995. As a global institution aimed at promoting international trade and economic cooperation, the WTO has adapted and transformed itself to meet the challenges posed by globalization and the changing dynamics of the global economy.

Initially, the predecessor of the WTO, the General Agreement on Tariffs and Trade (GATT), was established in 1947 to regulate international trade and reduce trade barriers. However, the GATT lacked enforcement mechanisms and its scope was limited to trade in goods. Recognizing the need for a more comprehensive and enforceable framework, negotiations among member countries led to the establishment of the WTO.

One of the crucial aspects of the WTO's evolution has been the inclusion of services and intellectual property rights within its scope. With the rise of the service sector and the increasing importance of intellectual property in the global economy, the WTO recognized the need to address these areas. As a result, the General Agreement on Trade in Services (GATS) and the Agreement on Trade-Related Aspects of Intellectual Property Rights (TRIPS) were incorporated into the WTO framework.

Another significant development in the evolution of the WTO has been the increased participation of developing countries. Historically, the WTO has been criticized for favoring the interests of developed countries, leading to concerns about its legitimacy and effectiveness. In response, the WTO has made efforts to address the concerns of developing countries by providing technical assistance, capacity building, and special and differential treatment provisions. These measures have aimed to ensure that the benefits of globalization and international trade are more evenly distributed.

Furthermore, the WTO has embraced the role of non-governmental organizations (NGOs) in influencing its policies and decisions. Recognizing the importance of diverse perspectives and public participation, the WTO has created platforms for dialogue and engagement with NGOs. This has allowed for a more inclusive and transparent decision-making process.

The WTO's role in resolving trade disputes has also evolved over time. The Dispute Settlement Mechanism (DSM) of the WTO has become a cornerstone of the organization, providing a transparent and rules-based system for resolving trade disputes between member countries. The DSM has played a crucial role in ensuring that trade disputes are resolved in a fair and equitable manner, thereby enhancing the credibility and effectiveness of the WTO.

Moreover, the WTO has taken significant steps towards promoting sustainable development. Recognizing the interlinkages between trade and the environment, the WTO has integrated environmental considerations into its rules and agreements. This has led to the establishment of the Committee on Trade and Environment (CTE) and the recognition of the importance of sustainable development in the WTO's mandate.

In conclusion, the evolution of the World Trade Organization has been marked by its adaptation to the challenges posed by globalization and the changing dynamics of the global economy. From its origins as the GATT, the WTO has expanded its scope to include services and intellectual property rights, increased the participation of developing countries, engaged with NGOs, resolved trade disputes, promoted sustainable development, and addressed various other issues related to labor rights, gender equality, fair trade practices, agricultural subsidies, and food security. These developments have reinforced the WTO's role as a key institution in shaping the rules of international trade and promoting global economic cooperation.

The Functions of the World Trade Organization

The World Trade Organization (WTO) is an international organization that plays a crucial role in shaping global trade. It serves as a forum for member countries to negotiate and establish trade rules, resolve disputes, and promote fair and open trade practices. This subchapter will explore the various functions of the WTO and its impact on different aspects of global trade.

One of the primary functions of the WTO is to provide a platform for member countries to negotiate trade agreements. Through its various rounds of negotiations, such as the Doha Round, the WTO facilitates discussions on various trade-related issues, including tariffs, subsidies, and market access. These negotiations aim to create a level playing field for all member countries and promote free and fair trade.

The WTO also serves as a forum for resolving trade disputes. Member countries can bring their trade grievances to the WTO, and a dispute settlement system is in place to address these issues. This system ensures that trade disputes are resolved in a fair and impartial manner, thereby promoting stability and predictability in global trade.

In addition to negotiations and dispute settlement, the WTO plays a crucial role in promoting sustainable development. It recognizes the importance of balancing economic growth with environmental protection and social development. The WTO encourages member countries to integrate environmental and social concerns into their trade policies, thus promoting sustainable trade practices.

Furthermore, the WTO is actively involved in promoting intellectual property rights (IPR) and patent protection. It provides a framework for member countries to protect and enforce IPR, which is essential for promoting innovation and creativity. By protecting IPR, the WTO encourages investment in research and development, leading to economic growth and technological advancement.

Moreover, the WTO aims to promote gender equality in international trade. It recognizes the importance of empowering women and promoting their participation in trade. Through various initiatives and capacity-building programs, the WTO works towards creating a more inclusive and gender-responsive trading system.

In conclusion, the World Trade Organization plays a vital role in shaping global trade. Its functions include negotiating trade agreements, resolving disputes, promoting sustainable development, protecting intellectual property rights, and promoting fair trade practices. By fulfilling these functions, the WTO contributes to economic growth, stability, and the overall well-being of member countries.

The Strengths of the World Trade Organization

The World Trade Organization (WTO) has emerged as a crucial global institution in the realm of international trade. Over the years, it has exhibited several strengths that have further solidified its importance. Understanding these strengths is essential for journalists, educators, scholars, politicians, diplomats, economists, legislators, and the public to grasp the significance and impact of the WTO.

One of the primary strengths of the WTO lies in its history. Established in 1995, the WTO succeeded the General Agreement on Tariffs and Trade (GATT) and has since become the only international organization dealing with the global rules of trade. Its long-standing presence in the international trade arena has allowed it to garner immense credibility and trust among its member nations.

The functioning of the WTO is another area where it showcases its strengths. The organization operates on the principle of consensus-based decision-making. This means that all member nations have an equal say in the decision-making process, regardless of their economic size or political influence. Such a democratic approach ensures that the interests of both developed and developing countries are taken into consideration, promoting a fair and inclusive global trading system.

Moreover, the WTO's dispute settlement mechanism is a significant strength. The organization offers a robust and impartial platform for resolving trade disputes among member nations. This mechanism encourages dialogue and negotiation, preventing trade wars and ensuring stability in global trade relations. The WTO's dispute settlement system is considered one of its most successful achievements, providing a rules-based framework for resolving conflicts.

Furthermore, the WTO plays a pivotal role in promoting sustainable development. Recognizing the interconnectedness of trade and environmental concerns, the organization has established various agreements and initiatives to address environmental sustainability. It encourages member nations to adopt measures that promote sustainable practices and discourages trade practices that harm the environment. By integrating sustainability into global trade, the WTO contributes to the overall welfare of societies and the planet.

In conclusion, the strengths of the World Trade Organization are multifaceted. Its rich history, consensus-based decision-making, robust dispute settlement mechanism, and commitment to sustainable development make it a crucial global institution. As globalization continues to shape the world economy, understanding the strengths of the WTO is pivotal in comprehending its impact on various aspects, such as labor rights, intellectual property, fair trade practices, agricultural subsidies, and gender equality in international trade. Journalists, educators, scholars, politicians, diplomats, economists, legislators, and the public must recognize and appreciate the strengths of the WTO to effectively engage with and assess its impact on the global trading system.

The Weaknesses of the World Trade Organization

The World Trade Organization (WTO) has played a significant role in regulating international trade and promoting global economic growth. However, it is not without its weaknesses. In this subchapter, we will explore some of the key weaknesses of the WTO that need to be addressed for a fairer and more inclusive global trading system.

One of the major weaknesses of the WTO is its decision-making process. The organization operates on a consensus-based approach, which means that all member countries must agree on any new rules or changes to existing ones. This can lead to significant delays and impede the progress of negotiations. Developing countries, in particular, often feel marginalized and disadvantaged in this process, as they lack the resources and expertise to effectively participate and influence the decision-making.

Another weakness is the unequal power dynamics within the WTO. Developed countries, especially the United States and European Union, hold substantial influence and often set the agenda. This can result in biased outcomes that favor the interests of these powerful nations, neglecting the needs and concerns of developing countries. The lack of representation and voice for smaller economies undermines the legitimacy of the WTO and hampers its ability to address global trade issues effectively.

Furthermore, the WTO's dispute settlement mechanism has faced criticism for being slow, costly, and complex. Resolving trade disputes can take several years, and the process heavily favors wealthier countries with the resources to navigate the legal complexities. This creates a sense of injustice and undermines the credibility of the WTO as a fair arbiter in trade conflicts.

The WTO's impact on labor rights and workers' rights is another weak area. While the organization has made some efforts to address these issues, there are limited mechanisms to enforce labor standards and ensure fair working conditions. This can lead to a race to the bottom, where countries compete by lowering labor standards to attract investment, resulting in a race to the bottom in terms of worker protections.

In conclusion, the weaknesses of the WTO need to be acknowledged and addressed to ensure a more inclusive and equitable global trading system. Reforms should focus on improving decision-making processes, giving developing countries a greater voice, and strengthening mechanisms to protect labor rights. By addressing these weaknesses, the

WTO can better fulfill its mandate of promoting fair and sustainable global trade.

Chapter 2: The Role of Developing Countries in the World Trade Organization

The Participation of Developing Countries in the World Trade Organization

The World Trade Organization (WTO) plays a crucial role in promoting global trade and economic development. As an international organization that regulates and facilitates trade between nations, the WTO aims to create a fair and transparent trading system that benefits all member countries. Developing countries, in particular, have become increasingly involved in the WTO over the years, as they recognize the importance of participating in global trade and reaping its benefits.

Developing countries make up a significant portion of the WTO's membership, and their participation is vital for the organization to fulfill its mandate effectively. These countries bring unique perspectives and interests to the negotiating table, ensuring that the WTO's policies and agreements take into account the specific challenges and needs of developing economies. By actively engaging in the WTO's decision-making processes, developing countries have the opportunity to influence global trade rules and shape the international trading system.

The involvement of developing countries in the WTO is not without its challenges. These nations often face capacity constraints, limited resources, and a lack of experience in trade negotiations, which can hinder their effective participation. However, the WTO has recognized the importance of addressing these barriers and has implemented various capacity-building initiatives to support developing countries in enhancing their trade-related capabilities.

Furthermore, the WTO provides a platform for developing countries to voice their concerns and advocate for their interests. Through the WTO's committees, councils, and dispute settlement mechanism, developing countries can raise issues related to trade barriers, market access, and unfair practices. This enables them to challenge trade measures that negatively impact their economies and seek resolution through a rules-based system.

The participation of developing countries in the WTO is not only crucial for their economic development but also for the overall effectiveness and legitimacy of the organization. Their involvement ensures that the WTO's policies and decisions reflect the diverse needs and aspirations of its membership. It also fosters a more inclusive and equitable global trading system, where developing countries can benefit from the opportunities provided by globalization.

In conclusion, the participation of developing countries in the World Trade Organization is essential for the organization to fulfill its objectives and promote global economic development. Despite the challenges they face, developing countries have increasingly engaged with the WTO, bringing their unique perspectives and interests to the table. Through their active involvement, these nations have the opportunity to shape global trade rules, address trade barriers, and advocate for their economic interests. The WTO, in turn, must continue to support and strengthen the participation of developing countries through capacity-building initiatives and inclusive decision-making processes. By doing so, the organization can ensure that the benefits of globalization are accessible to all, leading to a more prosperous and equitable world.

Challenges Faced by Developing Countries in the World Trade Organization

The World Trade Organization (WTO) serves as a platform for international trade negotiations, dispute settlement mechanisms, and the promotion of fair trade practices. However, developing countries face several challenges within the WTO that hinder their ability to fully participate and benefit from the global trading system.

One of the primary challenges faced by developing countries in the WTO is the power imbalance. Developed countries possess greater resources, expertise, and bargaining power, which often leads to unequal negotiations and decision-making processes. This power asymmetry can result in developing countries being marginalized and their interests overlooked.

Another challenge is the complexity of WTO rules and regulations. Developing countries often lack the capacity to fully understand and implement these rules, which can put them at a disadvantage. The technical barriers and legal complexities within the WTO can hinder their ability to effectively participate in negotiations and take advantage of trade opportunities.

Furthermore, developing countries face difficulties in accessing markets due to trade barriers imposed by developed countries. Tariffs, non-tariff barriers, and restrictions on agricultural subsidies limit the market access for developing countries' goods and services. This undermines their ability to compete on a level playing field and hampers their economic growth and development.

Additionally, the WTO's focus on trade liberalization can have adverse effects on developing countries. Opening up their markets to global competition can lead to job losses, decline in domestic industries, and increased dependency on imports. Developing countries often lack the necessary support mechanisms to mitigate these negative impacts, which can result in social and economic instability.

Moreover, the decision-making processes within the WTO often lack transparency and inclusivity. Developing countries often find it challenging to have their voices heard and their concerns addressed. This lack of representation and participation can undermine the legitimacy and effectiveness of the WTO.

To address these challenges, it is crucial for the WTO to prioritize the needs and interests of developing countries. This can be achieved by enhancing technical assistance and capacity-building programs to support developing countries in understanding and implementing WTO rules. Additionally, the WTO should promote fair and equitable negotiations, ensuring that the voices of developing countries are heard and their concerns are addressed.

Furthermore, developed countries should take steps to reduce trade barriers and provide market access opportunities for developing countries. This can be done through the elimination of tariffs, reduction of non-tariff barriers, and providing support for the development of domestic industries.

In conclusion, developing countries face numerous challenges within the WTO that hinder their ability to fully participate and benefit from the global trading system. Addressing these challenges requires a more inclusive and transparent decision-making process, enhanced technical assistance, and capacity-building support, as well as efforts to reduce trade barriers and promote fair trade practices. By addressing these challenges, the WTO can play a more effective role in promoting the economic development and well-being of developing countries.

Developing Countries' Influence on Decision-Making Processes

In the ever-evolving landscape of globalization, developing countries have emerged as key players in decision-making processes within the World Trade Organization (WTO). This subchapter delves into the significant influence of developing countries on shaping policies, regulations, and agreements within the WTO, and the implications of their participation for global trade.

Historically, the WTO has been dominated by developed countries, with decision-making power concentrated in their hands. However, the rise of developing countries, such as China, India, and Brazil, has challenged this imbalance. These countries, representing a substantial portion of the world's population and economic growth, have effectively asserted their interests and agendas, reshaping the dynamics of the WTO.

Developing countries have been instrumental in highlighting the need for fair and inclusive trade practices. Their participation has brought attention to issues such as agricultural subsidies, intellectual property rights, and labor standards. By advocating for their concerns, developing countries have pushed for reforms that promote sustainable development, gender equality, and workers' rights, thus addressing some of the weaknesses of the WTO.

Furthermore, developing countries have formed alliances and coalitions, strengthening their collective voice and negotiating power within the WTO. Through these alliances, they have successfully challenged the dominance of developed countries and influenced decision-making processes in their favor. This shift in power dynamics has led to a more balanced representation of interests and priorities in global trade discussions.

However, challenges persist. Developing countries often face resource constraints and capacity limitations, limiting their ability to fully engage in and influence decision-making processes. The dominance of developed countries in terms of resources, expertise, and influence continues to present hurdles for developing countries to overcome.

To address these challenges, it is crucial for developed countries to recognize and support the meaningful participation of developing countries in decision-making processes. Capacity-building initiatives, technical assistance, and financial support can help level the playing field and empower developing countries to fully engage in shaping global trade policies.

In conclusion, developing countries' influence on decision-making processes within the WTO has grown significantly in recent years. Their participation has brought attention to critical issues, challenged the dominance of developed countries, and pushed for reforms that promote fairness, sustainability, and inclusivity. However, ongoing efforts are needed to address the existing imbalance and ensure that developing countries have an equal say in shaping the future of global trade. The collective efforts of journalists, educators, scholars, politicians, diplomats, economists, legislators, and the public are essential in promoting a more equitable and inclusive WTO.

Efforts to Address the Needs of Developing Countries in the World Trade Organization

The World Trade Organization (WTO) has recognized the importance of addressing the needs of developing countries, given their unique challenges and vulnerabilities in the global economy. Efforts have been made to ensure that these countries are able to participate fully and effectively in the global trading system, allowing them to reap the benefits of globalization. This subchapter will explore the various initiatives and measures taken by the WTO to address the needs of developing countries.

One of the key efforts made by the WTO is the principle of special and differential treatment (SDT) for developing countries. SDT recognizes that developing countries may require different treatment compared to developed countries due to their limited capacity and resources. It allows for flexibility in implementing WTO agreements, such as longer transition periods and technical assistance, to ensure that developing countries can fully comply with their obligations.

The WTO has also taken steps to enhance the participation of developing countries in the decision-making process. The Committee on Trade and Development serves as a platform for developing countries to voice their concerns and interests. Regular meetings and consultations provide an opportunity for these countries to contribute to the formulation of trade policies and discuss issues that are of particular importance to them.

In addition, the WTO has established various capacity-building programs and technical assistance to help developing countries strengthen their trade-related infrastructure and institutions. These programs aim to enhance their ability to participate effectively in trade negotiations, implement WTO agreements, and integrate into the global trading system. Special attention is given to the needs of least-developed countries (LDCs), which face greater challenges in terms of capacity and resources.

Furthermore, the WTO has sought to address the imbalances in agricultural trade that disproportionately affect developing countries. The Agreement on Agriculture aims to promote fair and market-oriented agricultural trade, reduce trade-distorting subsidies, and improve market access for agricultural products from developing countries. Special provisions have been made to protect the food security and livelihoods of small-scale farmers in developing countries.

While these efforts have been commendable, it is important to note that challenges remain. Developing countries continue to face barriers in accessing markets, particularly in the agricultural and manufacturing sectors. The WTO must continue to work towards reducing these barriers and ensuring that the needs and interests of developing countries are adequately addressed.

In conclusion, the WTO recognizes the importance of addressing the needs of developing countries in the global trading system. Through initiatives such as special and differential treatment, capacity-building programs, and addressing imbalances in agricultural trade, efforts have been made to enhance the participation and benefits of developing countries in the WTO. However, ongoing efforts are required to ensure that the needs and concerns of developing countries are adequately addressed, allowing them to fully integrate into the global economy and benefit from globalization.

Chapter 3: The Impact of Globalization on the World Trade Organization

Globalization and Its Effects on International Trade

In today's interconnected world, globalization has become a driving force behind international trade. The concept of globalization refers to the increasing integration of economies, cultures, and societies across the globe. This subchapter will delve into the effects of globalization on international trade, shedding light on its implications for various stakeholders such as the World Trade Organization (WTO), developing countries, non-governmental organizations (NGOs), labor rights, sustainable development, intellectual property rights, fair trade practices, agricultural subsidies, food security, and gender equality.

Globalization has significantly impacted the World Trade Organization, an international body established to promote free and fair trade between nations. As the global economy becomes more interconnected, the WTO has faced new challenges in addressing trade disputes and ensuring a level playing field for all countries. The subchapter will explore the history, functions, strengths, and weaknesses of the WTO in light of globalization.

Developing countries play a crucial role in the WTO and are often disadvantaged by the asymmetrical nature of globalization. The subchapter will examine the impact of globalization on developing countries, highlighting the opportunities and challenges they face in participating in the global trading system.

NGOs have emerged as influential actors in shaping the policies and practices of the WTO. This subchapter will explore the role of non-governmental organizations in influencing the decision-making processes of the WTO, emphasizing their efforts to promote transparency, inclusivity, and sustainability in international trade.

Globalization has had implications for labor rights and workers' rights worldwide. The subchapter will analyze the impact of the WTO on labor rights, examining the organization's efforts to balance economic growth with social justice and fair working conditions.

Sustainable development has become a key concern in the era of globalization. The subchapter will discuss the WTO's role in promoting sustainable development, examining its efforts to reconcile economic growth with environmental protection and social welfare.

Intellectual property rights and patent protection have gained prominence in the era of globalization. The subchapter will explore the influence of the WTO on intellectual property rights, analyzing its role in balancing the interests of innovators and the public in a globalized economy.

Fair trade practices have become a pressing issue in the era of globalization. The subchapter will examine the WTO's role in promoting fair trade practices, addressing issues such as anti-dumping measures, subsidies, and trade barriers.

Agricultural subsidies and food security have been deeply affected by globalization. The subchapter will analyze the impact of the WTO on agricultural subsidies and food security, discussing the organization's efforts to ensure a fair and sustainable agricultural trade system.

Lastly, the subchapter will explore the WTO's role in promoting gender equality in international trade. It will shed light on the organization's efforts to address gender disparities, promote women's empowerment, and ensure women's meaningful participation in global trade.

Overall, this subchapter aims to provide a comprehensive understanding of the effects of globalization on international trade, while addressing the concerns and interests of various stakeholders such as the WTO, developing countries, NGOs, labor rights, sustainable development, intellectual property rights, fair trade practices, agricultural subsidies, food security, and gender equality. It is intended to appeal to journalists, educators, scholars, politicians, diplomats, economists, legislators, and the public.

The Role of the World Trade Organization in Globalization

Globalization has become an undeniable force shaping the modern world. As countries become increasingly interconnected through trade and investment, it has become crucial to establish rules and regulations to ensure fair and equitable economic exchanges. The World Trade Organization (WTO) plays a pivotal role in this process, acting as a global forum for trade negotiations, settling disputes, and setting standards for international trade.

The WTO, established in 1995, has a rich history of facilitating global trade by promoting transparency, predictability, and stability in the international economic system. Its primary function is to provide a platform for member countries to negotiate and reduce trade barriers, such as tariffs and quotas, thereby promoting free and open trade. By eliminating discriminatory practices and fostering a level playing field, the WTO has contributed significantly to the growth of global commerce.

One of the key strengths of the WTO lies in its inclusivity, ensuring that both developed and developing countries have a voice in shaping global trade policies. Developing countries, in particular, play a crucial role in the WTO, as it acts as a platform for them to articulate their interests and concerns. Through various mechanisms such as special and differential treatment, the WTO aims to promote the integration of developing countries into the global trading system, enabling them to reap the benefits of globalization.

However, the impact of globalization on the WTO cannot be overlooked. The rapid pace of economic integration and technological advancements has presented new challenges for the organization. The WTO must adapt to the changing dynamics of global trade, addressing emerging issues such as digital trade, intellectual property rights, and sustainable development.

The role of non-governmental organizations (NGOs) in influencing the WTO cannot be underestimated. NGOs bring diverse perspectives and expertise to the table, advocating for social, environmental, and labor rights within the realm of international trade. Their influence has been instrumental in shaping the WTO's agenda, ensuring that trade policies are not just economically beneficial but also socially and environmentally responsible.

The WTO also plays a crucial role in resolving trade disputes. Its dispute settlement mechanism provides a fair and transparent platform for members to settle their differences in a rules-based manner. This mechanism has been instrumental in preventing trade wars and promoting peaceful resolutions.

Moreover, the WTO has a significant impact on labor rights and workers' rights. It promotes the core labor standards established by the International Labor Organization, ensuring that trade does not come at the expense of workers' rights. The WTO also recognizes the importance of sustainable development, integrating environmental considerations into its trade policies.

Furthermore, the WTO plays a vital role in promoting fair trade practices. It combats unfair trade practices such as dumping and subsidies, ensuring a level playing field for all members. This fosters trust and confidence in the global trading system, promoting healthy competition and economic growth.

The WTO's influence extends to intellectual property rights and patent protection. By establishing international standards and enforcing intellectual property rules, the WTO encourages innovation and technological advancements, benefiting both developed and developing countries.

Agricultural subsidies and food security are critical issues in global trade, and the WTO plays a central role in addressing them. Through negotiations and agreements, the WTO seeks to strike a balance between the interests of agricultural producers and the need to ensure food security for all.

Finally, the WTO recognizes the importance of gender equality in international trade. It seeks to address gender disparities and empower women by promoting their participation in trade and addressing discriminatory practices.

In conclusion, the World Trade Organization plays a vital role in the process of globalization. As a global forum for trade negotiations and dispute settlement, it promotes free and fair trade, while considering the interests of all members. By addressing emerging challenges and promoting sustainable development, the WTO ensures that globalization benefits all stakeholders. Its impact on labor rights, fair trade practices, intellectual property rights, and gender equality cannot be overstated. However, the organization also faces weaknesses and must continuously adapt to the evolving global landscape.

Challenges Posed by Globalization to the World Trade Organization

Globalization has undoubtedly transformed the world economy, with the World Trade Organization (WTO) at the forefront of regulating and facilitating international trade. However, this rapid integration of economies has presented the WTO with a myriad of challenges that it must navigate to remain effective in the face of globalization.

One of the primary challenges the WTO faces is ensuring the inclusivity and representation of developing countries. Historically, developed countries have dominated the decision-making process within the organization, leading to concerns of inequality and marginalization. As globalization continues to reshape the global economic landscape, the WTO must address these power imbalances and empower developing countries to actively participate in shaping trade policies.

Furthermore, the impact of globalization on the WTO itself cannot be ignored. The organization must adapt to the changing dynamics of the global economy, including the rise of emerging markets and the rapid advancement of technology. Globalization has also given rise to non-state actors, such as non-governmental organizations (NGOs), who have increasingly sought to influence the WTO's decision-making process. The challenge for the WTO is to strike a balance between engaging with these stakeholders while maintaining its core principles of transparency and inclusivity.

Trade disputes have become more complex and multifaceted in the era of globalization. The WTO plays a crucial role in resolving these disputes through its dispute settlement mechanism. However, the organization faces challenges in ensuring timely and effective resolution, especially with the growing number of disputes involving intellectual property rights, patent protection, and fair trade practices. The WTO needs to strengthen its dispute settlement mechanism to address these challenges and maintain its credibility as the global arbiter of trade disputes.

Additionally, globalization has brought attention to labor rights, workers' rights, and sustainable development. Critics argue that the WTO's focus on free trade has come at the expense of labor and environmental standards. The organization must adapt to these concerns by incorporating social and environmental considerations into its trade policies, promoting fair trade practices, and addressing the impact of trade on labor rights, workers' rights, and sustainable development.

Moreover, the WTO's role in intellectual property rights and patent protection has become increasingly significant in the era of globalization. As technology and innovation continue to drive economic growth, the organization must ensure that intellectual property rights are adequately protected while also balancing the interests of developing countries in accessing affordable medicines and technology transfer.

Lastly, the WTO has a crucial role to play in addressing agricultural subsidies and food security. In an era of globalization, agricultural trade has become highly distorted due to subsidies provided by some countries, leading to concerns of unfair competition and food insecurity. The organization must work towards a fair and equitable agricultural trade regime that addresses the challenges posed by globalization and ensures food security for all.

In conclusion, the challenges posed by globalization to the World Trade Organization are numerous and complex. From ensuring the representation of developing countries to addressing labor rights, sustainable development, and fair trade practices, the WTO must adapt to the evolving global economic landscape. By effectively addressing these challenges, the WTO can continue to play a crucial role in promoting global trade that is inclusive, sustainable, and beneficial for all.

Adapting to Globalization: Reforms and Adjustments within the World Trade Organization

In this subchapter, we will delve into the crucial topic of how the World Trade Organization (WTO) has been adapting to the challenges posed by globalization. As the world becomes increasingly interconnected and economies become more interdependent, it is imperative for the WTO to continually reform and adjust its policies and mechanisms to ensure a fair and sustainable global trading system.

Globalization has brought about significant changes in the world economy, with both positive and negative impacts on various aspects of international trade. The WTO has recognized the need to address these impacts and has undertaken important reforms to maintain its relevance and effectiveness in the face of globalization.

One key area of reform is the inclusion of developing countries in the decision-making processes of the WTO. Historically, developing countries have had limited influence within the organization, often being marginalized in negotiations. However, recognizing the importance of their participation, the WTO has implemented measures to enhance their representation and voice. This includes capacity-building programs and technical assistance to help developing countries effectively engage in trade negotiations.

Moreover, the WTO has also been working towards addressing the challenges posed by globalization on labor rights and workers' rights. It has placed emphasis on promoting fair and decent work conditions, as well as ensuring that trade liberalization does not lead to exploitation or the erosion of labor standards.

Another critical aspect of the WTO's adaptation to globalization is its role in promoting sustainable development. Recognizing the environmental consequences of increased global trade, the WTO has integrated sustainable development principles into its policies. This includes encouraging the use of environmentally friendly technologies, promoting the conservation of natural resources, and ensuring that trade does not undermine environmental protection measures.

Additionally, the WTO has been actively involved in shaping intellectual property rights and patent protection in the era of globalization. It has sought to strike a balance between protecting intellectual property rights and promoting access to affordable medicines, particularly in developing countries.

Furthermore, the WTO has played a significant role in promoting fair trade practices. It has worked towards reducing trade barriers, eliminating discriminatory practices, and encouraging transparency and predictability in trade relations.

Lastly, the WTO has recognized the importance of addressing agricultural subsidies and food security issues. It has sought to strike a balance between supporting agricultural subsidies for developing countries and ensuring that they do not distort international trade. Additionally, the WTO has been actively involved in promoting gender equality in international trade, recognizing the pivotal role of women in global economic development.

In conclusion, the WTO has been proactive in adapting to the challenges brought about by globalization. Through reforms and adjustments, it has strived to ensure that the benefits of globalization are distributed equitably, while mitigating its negative impacts. By actively engaging with stakeholders, addressing labor rights, promoting sustainable development, and advocating for fair trade practices, the WTO continues to play a crucial role in shaping the global trading system in a manner that benefits all nations and promotes inclusivity and sustainability.

Chapter 4: The Role of Non-Governmental Organizations in Influencing the World Trade Organization

The Rise of Non-Governmental Organizations in Global Governance

In recent decades, the influence of non-governmental organizations (NGOs) in global governance has experienced a remarkable rise. These organizations, which are independent of government control and driven by the pursuit of common goals, have become key players in shaping policies and decision-making processes on a global scale. This subchapter will delve into the reasons behind the ascent of NGOs in global governance, specifically focusing on their impact on the World Trade Organization (WTO).

NGOs have emerged as significant actors in global governance due to several factors. Firstly, the increasing interconnectedness and interdependence of nations in the era of globalization have created opportunities for NGOs to address global issues that transcend national boundaries. This has allowed NGOs to fill gaps in governance left by traditional state-centric institutions like the WTO.

Secondly, NGOs have gained prominence through their ability to mobilize public opinion and raise awareness about pressing social, economic, and environmental concerns. Their advocacy efforts often challenge the status quo and push governments and international organizations like the WTO to take action.

Regarding the WTO, NGOs have played a crucial role in influencing its decision-making processes. They have actively engaged in WTO meetings, submitted position papers, and organized campaigns to promote transparency, accountability, and inclusivity within the organization. By providing alternative viewpoints and expertise, NGOs have contributed to more informed deliberations and broadened the scope of discussions at the WTO.

NGOs have also been instrumental in shaping specific policy areas within the WTO. For instance, they have brought attention to labor rights and workers' rights, intellectual property rights and patent protection, fair trade practices, and gender equality in international trade. Through their research, advocacy, and monitoring efforts, NGOs have pushed for reforms and greater consideration of these issues in WTO agreements and negotiations.

However, the rise of NGOs in global governance has not been without challenges. Some critics argue that NGOs lack democratic legitimacy and accountability, as they are not elected or directly accountable to the public. Moreover, their growing influence has led to concerns about their capture by powerful interest groups or the corporatization of civil society.

In conclusion, the rise of NGOs in global governance, particularly their impact on the WTO, has been a transformative development in recent years. Their ability to mobilize public opinion, provide alternative perspectives, and advocate for various social, economic, and environmental concerns has made them indispensable actors in shaping global policies. However, it is essential to strike a balance between the influence of NGOs and the accountability and legitimacy of state-centric institutions like the WTO. By recognizing and harnessing the strengths of NGOs while addressing the challenges they pose, global governance can become more inclusive, responsive, and effective in addressing the complex challenges of the 21st century.

Non-Governmental Organizations' Engagement with the World Trade Organization

Non-Governmental Organizations (NGOs) play a crucial role in shaping international trade policies and influencing the decision-making process of the World Trade Organization (WTO). Comprised of various stakeholders, including civil society groups, advocacy organizations, and industry associations, NGOs bring diverse perspectives and expertise to the table.

NGOs engage with the WTO in several ways, such as participating in public hearings, providing technical expertise, and submitting policy recommendations. Their involvement ensures that the voices of marginalized groups and communities are heard and considered in trade negotiations, making the process more inclusive and democratic.

One area where NGOs have had a significant impact is in advocating for the interests of developing countries. By providing research, analysis, and policy recommendations, NGOs help to level the playing field for these countries, which often face challenges in participating effectively in WTO negotiations. NGOs have pushed for reforms in the WTO's decision-making processes to ensure that developing countries have a greater say in shaping the global trading system.

Moreover, NGOs have been instrumental in highlighting the impact of globalization on various aspects of society, such as labor rights, workers' rights, and sustainable development. Through research, advocacy campaigns, and collaboration with grassroots organizations, NGOs have raised awareness about the social and environmental implications of trade policies. They have pushed for the inclusion of labor and environmental standards in trade agreements, ensuring that economic growth goes hand in hand with social progress and environmental sustainability.

NGOs have also played a pivotal role in addressing trade disputes. By providing legal expertise and monitoring the dispute settlement process, NGOs contribute to the transparency and fairness of the system. They have helped to resolve conflicts and promote peaceful resolution mechanisms, reducing the potential for trade wars and protectionism.

Furthermore, NGOs have been at the forefront of advocating for fair trade practices, intellectual property rights, patent protection, and gender equality in international trade. They have worked to ensure that trade policies do not undermine the rights of vulnerable communities or exploit their intellectual property. NGOs have called for greater transparency and accountability in trade negotiations and have promoted policies that promote fair and ethical trade practices.

In conclusion, NGOs are vital actors in shaping the policies and decision-making processes of the World Trade Organization. Their engagement helps to ensure that the WTO addresses the concerns of all stakeholders, especially those of developing countries, marginalized communities, and the environment. By providing expertise, advocacy, and research, NGOs contribute to a more inclusive, democratic, and sustainable global trading system. Their role in promoting fair trade practices, protecting labor rights, and advocating for sustainable development is crucial in the era of globalization.

The Influence of Non-Governmental Organizations on World Trade Organization Policies and Negotiations

Introduction:

Non-Governmental Organizations (NGOs) have emerged as significant actors in shaping global governance, including the policies and negotiations of the World Trade Organization (WTO). With an increasing ability to mobilize resources and advocate for specific causes, NGOs have managed to influence the decision-making processes and priorities of the WTO. This subchapter aims to explore the various ways in which NGOs impact the policies and negotiations of the WTO, highlighting both their strengths and limitations.

NGOs as Advocates for Developing Countries:

One of the key roles of NGOs in the WTO is to advocate for the interests of developing countries. By providing a platform for marginalized voices, NGOs have successfully brought attention to the unique challenges faced by developing nations in the global trading system. Their research, analysis, and lobbying efforts have pushed for reforms that address the imbalances and inequities in WTO policies.

Influencing Policy Debates:

NGOs play a crucial role in shaping policy debates within the WTO. By providing alternative perspectives, they challenge the dominant narratives and push for more inclusive and sustainable trade practices. Through their engagement with governments, scholars, and other stakeholders, NGOs bring forth evidence-based research and analysis that influence the decision-making processes of the WTO.

Monitoring and Accountability:

NGOs act as watchdogs, monitoring the implementation of WTO policies and holding governments accountable for their commitments. They provide independent assessments of the impact of trade policies on various sectors, including labor rights, the environment, and public health. By highlighting discrepancies between rhetoric and action, NGOs ensure that the WTO remains responsive to the concerns of the public and civil society.

Limitations and Challenges:

While NGOs have made significant contributions to the WTO, they face certain limitations and challenges. Their diverse interests and priorities often lead to disagreements and fragmentation within the NGO community. Additionally, the influence of NGOs is often constrained by power imbalances within the WTO, where developed countries exert greater control over decision-making processes.

Conclusion:

Non-Governmental Organizations have emerged as important actors in shaping World Trade Organization policies and negotiations. Their advocacy for developing countries, ability to influence policy debates, and role in monitoring and accountability have contributed to a more inclusive and responsive WTO. However, challenges remain, and further efforts are needed to enhance the influence of NGOs and ensure a fair and equitable global trading system. As journalists, educators, scholars, politicians, diplomats, economists, legislators, and the public, it is essential to engage with and critically analyze the role of NGOs in the WTO to promote transparency, accountability, and sustainable development.

Criticisms and Debates Surrounding Non-Governmental Organizations' Role in the World Trade Organization

Non-Governmental Organizations (NGOs) have emerged as important actors in global governance, and their role in influencing international institutions such as the World Trade Organization (WTO) has been a subject of much debate and criticism. This subchapter delves into the criticisms and debates surrounding NGOs' involvement in the WTO, examining both their potential benefits and challenges.

One of the key criticisms leveled against NGOs' role in the WTO is the lack of democratic representation. Critics argue that these organizations, often driven by their own agendas and interests, do not necessarily represent the broader public or the diverse range of stakeholders affected by WTO policies. This leads to concerns about the legitimacy and accountability of NGOs in shaping the organization's decisions.

Moreover, some argue that NGOs' participation in the WTO can be problematic due to their limited resources and expertise. While NGOs often bring valuable insights and perspectives to the table, their capacity to engage in complex negotiations and provide technical expertise may be limited. This raises questions about the extent to which NGOs can effectively contribute to the WTO's decision-making processes.

Another criticism revolves around the potential influence of NGOs on the WTO's agenda-setting. Critics argue that NGOs, which often advocate for specific social and environmental issues, may push the organization to prioritize these concerns over economic considerations. This can lead to an imbalance in the WTO's focus and detract from its primary mandate of promoting free and fair trade.

On the other hand, proponents of NGO involvement in the WTO highlight the important role these organizations play in bringing marginalized voices and perspectives to the table. NGOs often represent civil society groups, indigenous communities, and other marginalized stakeholders who may not have direct access to the WTO. Their participation can help ensure that the concerns of these groups are taken into account in trade negotiations and dispute settlements.

Furthermore, NGOs can serve as watchdogs, monitoring the actions of the WTO and pushing for greater transparency and accountability. By shining a light on the WTO's decision-making processes and promoting public debate, NGOs can help foster a more inclusive and democratic global trade system.

In conclusion, the role of NGOs in the WTO is a topic of ongoing debate and criticism. While there are concerns about representation, expertise, and agenda-setting, NGOs also bring valuable perspectives and serve as important checks and balances on the organization. Striking the right balance between their involvement and the need for effective governance remains a challenge for the WTO and the broader global community.

Chapter 5: The World Trade Organization's Role in Resolving Trade Disputes

The Dispute Settlement Mechanism of the World Trade Organization

The World Trade Organization (WTO) plays a crucial role in resolving trade disputes among its member countries. The Dispute Settlement Mechanism (DSM) of the WTO serves as a platform for settling these disputes in a fair and impartial manner. This subchapter will examine the functioning of the DSM and its significance in maintaining a rules-based global trading system.

The DSM is a unique feature of the WTO that distinguishes it from its predecessor, the General Agreement on Tariffs and Trade (GATT). It provides an effective means to enforce the rights and obligations of member countries under the WTO agreements. The DSM is based on a two-tiered system, consisting of a Dispute Settlement Body (DSB) and an Appellate Body (AB). The DSB, composed of representatives from all WTO member countries, oversees the dispute settlement process, while the AB acts as the final appellate authority.

One of the strengths of the DSM is its transparency. The entire dispute settlement process is conducted in a highly transparent manner, allowing interested parties, including journalists, educators, scholars, politicians, diplomats, economists, legislators, and the public, to closely follow the proceedings. This transparency ensures that the decisions reached by the DSB and AB are accountable and can be scrutinized by the global community.

Moreover, the DSM promotes the rule of law in international trade. By providing a forum for resolving trade disputes, the WTO ensures that countries abide by their commitments under the WTO agreements. This contributes to a more predictable and stable trading environment, which benefits all participants, particularly developing countries.

However, the DSM also has some weaknesses that need to be addressed. For instance, the AB is currently facing a crisis due to the United States' blocking of the appointment of new judges. This has resulted in a backlog of cases and undermines the effectiveness of the DSM. Additionally, the DSM has been criticized for being slow and costly, which can deter smaller countries from utilizing the mechanism.

In conclusion, the DSM of the WTO plays a vital role in resolving trade disputes and maintaining a rules-based global trading system. Its transparency and adherence to the rule of law make it an essential tool for journalists, educators, scholars, politicians, diplomats, economists, legislators, and the public to understand and assess the impact of trade disputes on the global economy. However, efforts should be made to address the weaknesses of the DSM to ensure its continued effectiveness and accessibility for all WTO member countries.

The Process of Resolving Trade Disputes within the World Trade Organization

Trade disputes are inevitable in the globalized world we live in today. As nations engage in international trade, conflicts arise due to differing interpretations of trade agreements, unfair trade practices, or violations of intellectual property rights. To maintain a fair and level playing field, the World Trade Organization (WTO) has established a robust process for resolving such disputes.

The process of resolving trade disputes within the WTO involves several stages aimed at encouraging dialogue, finding mutually agreeable solutions, and ensuring compliance with trade rules. It is a transparent and structured mechanism that upholds the principles of fairness, predictability, and stability in international trade.

The first step in resolving a trade dispute is consultation between the parties involved. The complaining party initiates this process by requesting consultations with the alleged violating party. The objective of these consultations is to reach a mutually satisfactory resolution within 60 days. If consultations fail to resolve the dispute, the complaining party may request the establishment of a panel.

The panel, composed of independent experts, is responsible for examining the dispute and issuing a ruling based on the relevant WTO agreements. The panel's decision is then submitted to the Dispute Settlement Body (DSB) for adoption. However, either party can appeal the panel's ruling within 60 days, leading to a review by the Appellate Body.

The Appellate Body, consisting of seven members, reviews the legal aspects of the panel's ruling and issues a final report. Its decisions are binding and must be adopted by the DSB unless there is a consensus against it. This robust dispute settlement mechanism ensures the impartiality and effectiveness of the WTO's dispute resolution process.

The WTO's dispute settlement system has been hailed as one of its greatest strengths. It provides a forum for resolving conflicts and upholding the principles of free and fair trade. By ensuring compliance with trade rules, the WTO promotes stability and predictability in the global trading system.

However, the process is not without its weaknesses. The Appellate Body has faced challenges, including a shortage of members, which has hindered its ability to handle disputes effectively. Moreover, the enforcement of rulings remains a concern, as some countries have been slow to comply with the decisions.

Despite these challenges, the WTO's dispute settlement process plays a crucial role in maintaining the integrity of the global trading system.

It provides a fair and transparent platform for resolving conflicts and upholding the rights and obligations of member countries. By fostering a rules-based trading environment, the WTO contributes to economic growth, stability, and development worldwide.

Criticisms and Challenges of the World Trade Organization's Dispute Settlement System

The World Trade Organization (WTO) has been widely criticized for various aspects of its dispute settlement system. While the system aims to provide a fair and efficient mechanism for resolving trade disputes among member countries, there are several issues that have been raised by critics.

One of the main criticisms is the perceived bias towards developed countries in the dispute settlement process. Developing countries often argue that the system favors wealthier nations, as they have more resources and legal expertise to navigate the complex procedures. This has led to concerns about unequal access to justice within the WTO.

Another challenge is the length and complexity of the dispute settlement process. Cases can take several years to reach a resolution, which can be detrimental to businesses and trade flows. Critics argue that this extended timeline undermines the effectiveness of the system and discourages smaller economies from pursuing their claims.

Moreover, some argue that the WTO's dispute settlement system lacks transparency. The process is primarily conducted behind closed doors, and only the final panel reports are made public. This has raised concerns about accountability and the ability of civil society organizations to monitor and participate in the process.

Additionally, there have been concerns about the enforcement of WTO rulings. While member countries are expected to comply with the decisions, there have been instances where countries have failed to do so without facing significant consequences. This undermines the credibility and effectiveness of the dispute settlement system.

Furthermore, critics argue that the system does not adequately address certain issues, such as environmental and labor standards. They believe that the narrow focus on trade-related disputes neglects the broader social and environmental impacts of international trade.

To address these criticisms and challenges, the WTO has made efforts to reform its dispute settlement system. These include initiatives to improve transparency, streamline procedures, and enhance the participation of developing countries. However, there is still a need for further reforms to ensure a fair and efficient system that addresses the concerns of all member countries.

In conclusion, while the WTO's dispute settlement system plays a crucial role in resolving trade disputes, it faces several criticisms and challenges. These include perceived bias towards developed countries, lengthy and complex procedures, lack of transparency, enforcement issues, and limited scope. As the WTO continues to evolve, it is essential to address these concerns and make necessary reforms to strengthen the credibility and effectiveness of the dispute settlement system.

Recent Case Studies of Trade Disputes and their Resolution

In this subchapter, we will explore several recent case studies of trade disputes and their resolution, highlighting the role played by the World Trade Organization (WTO) in addressing these conflicts. These case studies shed light on the effectiveness of the WTO's dispute settlement mechanism and its impact on various aspects of international trade.

One notable case study is the dispute between the United States and China over intellectual property rights (IPR) violations. The US accused China of unfair practices, including forced technology transfers and inadequate protection of IPR. The WTO played a crucial role in resolving this dispute by establishing a panel to examine the allegations and issuing a ruling in favor of the US. This ruling led to China adopting measures to strengthen IPR protection, thereby promoting fair trade practices.

Another case study involves the European Union's (EU) challenge against the United States' agricultural subsidies, particularly those granted to the cotton industry. The EU argued that these subsidies distorted global trade and harmed cotton producers in developing countries. The WTO's dispute settlement process facilitated negotiations between the two parties, resulting in a reduction of US subsidies and increased market access for cotton exporters from developing nations.

Additionally, the dispute between India and the United States over solar energy policies showcases the WTO's role in promoting sustainable development. India had implemented policies favoring domestic production of solar cells and modules, which the US claimed discriminated against foreign manufacturers. The WTO panel ruled in favor of the US, stating that India's measures violated WTO rules. As a result, India revised its policies to ensure non-discrimination and fair competition in the solar energy sector.

These case studies demonstrate the significance of the WTO's dispute settlement system in resolving trade conflicts and promoting fair trade practices. By providing a neutral platform for the resolution of disputes, the WTO contributes to the stability and predictability of the global trading system. Moreover, the WTO's rulings have a far-reaching impact on various aspects of international trade, including labor rights, intellectual property rights, gender equality, and sustainable development.

Journalists, educators, scholars, politicians, diplomats, economists, legislators, and the public should closely examine these case studies to understand the complexities of trade disputes and the role played by the WTO in resolving them. By doing so, they can gain valuable insights into the strengths and weaknesses of the WTO and contribute to the ongoing discussions on the impact of globalization on international trade and the future of the world trading system.

Chapter 6: The World Trade Organization's Impact on Labor Rights and Workers' Rights

The Relationship between Trade and Labor Standards

In the context of globalization and international trade, the relationship between trade and labor standards has become a topic of great importance and debate. This subchapter aims to explore the intricate connection between these two factors, shedding light on the various perspectives and implications for different stakeholders.

Trade, as facilitated by the World Trade Organization (WTO), has undoubtedly brought about numerous economic benefits, including increased productivity, job creation, and overall economic growth. However, concerns have been raised regarding the impact of trade on labor standards, particularly in developing countries.

On one hand, proponents argue that trade can act as a catalyst for improved labor standards. Increased trade can lead to enhanced competitiveness, encouraging countries to adopt higher labor standards to attract foreign investment and access global markets. Furthermore, trade agreements, such as those negotiated within the framework of the WTO, often include provisions promoting labor rights and prohibiting forced labor and child labor.

On the other hand, critics contend that trade liberalization may lead to a "race to the bottom" phenomenon, where countries lower their labor standards in order to attract investment and gain a competitive edge. This can result in exploitative labor practices, poor working conditions, and violations of workers' rights. Moreover, developing countries often face challenges in enforcing labor standards due to limited resources and weak institutional capacities.

To address these concerns, it is crucial to strike a balance between promoting trade and ensuring the protection of labor rights. The WTO, as the global governing body for trade, plays a significant role in this regard. It has established various mechanisms to address labor-related issues, including the Trade Policy Review Mechanism (TPRM) and the Technical Assistance and Training Program (TATP). These initiatives aim to promote dialogue, capacity-building, and technical assistance to help countries improve their labor standards.

Additionally, non-governmental organizations (NGOs) also play a vital role in influencing the WTO's approach to labor standards. They act as watchdogs, advocating for the inclusion of labor provisions in trade agreements and monitoring compliance with existing standards.

The relationship between trade and labor standards is complex and multi-faceted. It requires a comprehensive approach that considers the interests of all stakeholders involved. By promoting dialogue, capacity-building, and accountability, the WTO, together with NGOs and other actors, can strive towards a fair and sustainable global trading system that upholds labor rights and standards. It is through such collective efforts that the potential negative impacts of trade on labor can be mitigated, ensuring a more equitable and inclusive global economy.

The World Trade Organization's Efforts to Address Labor Rights and Workers' Rights

The World Trade Organization (WTO) has been making significant efforts to address labor rights and workers' rights in the context of globalization. As the world becomes increasingly interconnected, it is crucial to ensure that economic growth and international trade do not come at the expense of basic human rights.

Labor rights and workers' rights have become crucial aspects of the global trade agenda due to concerns about exploitative labor practices, poor working conditions, and unfair treatment of workers. The WTO recognizes the importance of incorporating social considerations into its trade policies to promote fair and sustainable development.

One of the key ways in which the WTO addresses labor rights is through its agreements and conventions. The organization has developed a set of principles known as the Fundamental Principles and Rights at Work, which include the freedom of association, the right to collective bargaining, the elimination of forced labor, the abolition of child labor, and the elimination of discrimination in employment. These principles serve as a foundation for member countries to protect and promote labor rights within their own jurisdictions.

Furthermore, the WTO encourages member countries to adhere to internationally recognized labor standards set by other organizations, such as the International Labour Organization (ILO). The ILO's core labor standards cover areas such as minimum wages, working hours, occupational safety and health, and equality in the workplace. By promoting compliance with these standards, the WTO aims to ensure that workers' rights are respected and protected in the global trading system.

In addition to its agreements and conventions, the WTO also provides a platform for member countries to discuss labor issues and exchange best practices. Through its regular meetings and committees, the organization facilitates dialogue on labor rights and workers' rights, allowing countries to learn from each other's experiences and improve their own policies and practices.

However, it is important to note that the WTO's efforts to address labor rights and workers' rights have faced criticisms. Some argue that the organization's focus on trade liberalization and market access may undermine labor standards, as countries might engage in a race to the bottom to attract investment by lowering labor standards. Others argue that the WTO's dispute settlement mechanism lacks teeth when it comes to enforcing labor rights.

Despite these challenges, the WTO remains committed to incorporating labor rights and workers' rights into the global trade agenda. By promoting the respect for labor standards and facilitating dialogue on labor issues, the organization aims to ensure that the benefits of globalization are shared equitably and sustainably.

Criticisms and Debates Surrounding the World Trade Organization's Approach to Labor Rights

The World Trade Organization (WTO) has been at the center of numerous discussions and debates regarding its approach to labor rights. Critics argue that the organization's policies and practices do not adequately protect workers' rights, leading to exploitation and unfair labor practices in many developing countries.

One of the main criticisms is that the WTO's focus on trade liberalization and market access has overshadowed labor rights concerns. The organization's primary objective is to promote free trade and remove barriers to international commerce. However, this emphasis on trade often comes at the expense of labor standards. Critics argue that the WTO's policies prioritize economic growth over workers' well-being, resulting in poor working conditions, low wages, and limited workers' rights protection.

Moreover, some argue that the WTO lacks effective mechanisms to enforce labor standards. While the organization has agreements in place that address labor rights, such as the Trade-Related Aspects of Intellectual Property Rights (TRIPS) agreement, these provisions are seen as weak and insufficient. Critics argue that the WTO should have stronger enforcement mechanisms to ensure that member countries adhere to labor rights standards.

Another debate surrounding the WTO's approach to labor rights is the role of non-governmental organizations (NGOs). NGOs play a significant role in influencing the organization's policies and advocating for labor rights. However, critics argue that the WTO does not give enough importance to the voices and concerns of these organizations. They claim that the organization lacks transparency and inclusivity in its decision-making processes, which hampers efforts to address labor rights adequately.

Furthermore, the impact of globalization on labor rights is a contentious issue. While proponents argue that globalization can lead to increased job opportunities and economic growth, critics claim that it often exacerbates inequality and exploitation. They argue that the WTO's policies have allowed multinational corporations to exploit cheap labor in developing countries, leading to a race to the bottom in terms of labor standards.

In conclusion, the WTO's approach to labor rights has faced significant criticism and debate. Critics argue that the organization's trade-focused agenda often neglects labor standards, resulting in exploitation and unfair labor practices. They call for stronger enforcement mechanisms and increased representation of NGOs in the decision-making processes. The impact of globalization on labor rights is also a contentious issue, with arguments highlighting both the potential benefits and negative consequences. As the world becomes increasingly interconnected, it is crucial to address these criticisms and debates to ensure that the WTO promotes fair trade practices and protects workers' rights.

Case Studies Highlighting the Intersection of Trade and Labor Rights within the World Trade Organization

In this subchapter, we will explore various case studies that shed light on the complex relationship between trade and labor rights within the World Trade Organization (WTO). These case studies exemplify the challenges faced by the WTO in reconciling the pursuit of free trade with the protection of workers' rights.

One such case study is the infamous 1999 WTO protests in Seattle, Washington, where activists from labor unions and non-governmental organizations (NGOs) voiced their concerns about the negative impact of globalization on workers' rights. This event highlighted the need for the WTO to address labor standards within its framework and sparked a global dialogue on the intersection of trade and labor rights.

Another case study involves the controversial use of labor standards as a non-tariff barrier to trade. Developing countries argue that developed countries use labor standards to protect their domestic industries and limit competition. This raises questions about the WTO's role in ensuring fair trade practices while respecting the diversity of labor standards across member states.

Furthermore, the case of the Rana Plaza tragedy in Bangladesh in 2013 demonstrates the urgent need for the WTO to address labor rights in the garment industry. The collapse of the Rana Plaza building, which housed several garment factories, resulted in the deaths of over a thousand workers. This incident highlighted the exploitative labor practices prevalent in the global supply chain and the responsibility of the WTO to promote decent working conditions.

Moreover, the ongoing debate surrounding the inclusion of labor rights in trade agreements, such as the Trans-Pacific Partnership (TPP), showcases the divergent views among member states. Some argue that labor rights should be an integral part of trade agreements to ensure a level playing field, while others contend that labor standards should be addressed through separate international agreements.

These case studies underscore the complex and multifaceted nature of the intersection between trade and labor rights within the WTO. They highlight the need for a nuanced approach that takes into account the diverse perspectives of member states, the role of non-governmental organizations, and the imperative to promote sustainable development and fair trade practices.

Ultimately, addressing the intersection of trade and labor rights is crucial for the WTO to fulfill its mandate of promoting global economic growth while safeguarding the welfare of workers worldwide. The case studies presented in this subchapter provide valuable insights into the ongoing debates and challenges in this area, aiming to stimulate further discussion among journalists, educators, scholars, politicians, diplomats, economists, legislators, and the public.

Chapter 7: The World Trade Organization's Role in Promoting Sustainable Development

The Concept of Sustainable Development in the Context of International Trade

Sustainable development has emerged as a key concept in the realm of international trade, with the understanding that economic growth should not come at the expense of environmental degradation and social inequality. This subchapter aims to explore the concept of sustainable development within the context of international trade, and its implications for the world trade organization (WTO) and its member states.

In recent decades, globalization has led to an increase in international trade, facilitated by the WTO. However, concerns have been raised about the negative impacts of this trade on the environment and society. Sustainable development seeks to address these concerns by promoting a balance between economic growth, social development, and environmental preservation.

The WTO, as the global governing body for international trade, has recognized the importance of sustainable development and has integrated it into its policies and practices. The organization acknowledges that trade should contribute to sustainable development and has made efforts to promote this through various means.

One of the key ways in which the WTO promotes sustainable development is through the consideration of environmental and social factors in trade agreements. The organization encourages its member states to incorporate sustainable development principles into their trade policies, such as the use of environmental impact assessments and the promotion of labor rights.

Furthermore, the WTO has played a role in addressing trade-related environmental issues, such as the trade in environmentally sensitive goods and services. The organization has facilitated negotiations on environmental agreements, such as the Trade and Environment Committee, which aims to promote the integration of environmental concerns into trade rules.

However, critics argue that the WTO's efforts towards sustainable development have been insufficient. They argue that the organization's focus on liberalizing trade may undermine environmental and social protections, particularly in developing countries. They also argue that the WTO's dispute settlement mechanism does not adequately consider sustainable development concerns.

In conclusion, the concept of sustainable development is essential in the context of international trade. The WTO plays a crucial role in promoting sustainable development through its policies and practices. However, there are ongoing debates and challenges regarding the organization's effectiveness in balancing economic growth with environmental and social concerns.

The World Trade Organization's Initiatives and Policies Supporting Sustainable Development

The World Trade Organization (WTO) has been actively engaged in promoting sustainable development through various initiatives and policies. Recognizing the importance of integrating economic, social, and environmental concerns, the WTO has made significant efforts to ensure that trade policies contribute to sustainable development goals.

One of the key initiatives by the WTO is the Trade and Environment Committee (TEC), which focuses on the relationship between trade and environmental issues. The TEC provides a platform for member countries to discuss and exchange information on trade-related environmental measures, such as the promotion of renewable energy, sustainable agriculture, and the conservation of biodiversity. Through this committee, the WTO aims to facilitate the integration of environmental considerations into trade policies.

Another important aspect of the WTO's efforts towards sustainable development is through the Trade and Development Committee (TDC). This committee addresses the concerns of developing countries, particularly in relation to their development needs and capacity-building. The TDC works towards ensuring that trade policies and agreements take into account the specific challenges faced by developing countries, including poverty eradication, access to essential services, and technology transfer for sustainable development.

Furthermore, the WTO's Aid for Trade initiative plays a crucial role in supporting sustainable development. This initiative aims to help developing countries build their capacity to participate in international trade and benefit from it. By providing financial and technical assistance, the WTO helps these countries enhance their infrastructure, improve trade-related skills, and integrate into global value chains, thus fostering sustainable economic growth and development.

In terms of policy, the WTO has also been actively involved in addressing environmental concerns through its agreements. For instance, the Agreement on Trade-Related Aspects of Intellectual Property Rights (TRIPS) includes provisions that allow governments to take measures to protect public health and the environment. Similarly, the Agreement on Agriculture includes provisions that promote sustainable agriculture practices and enhance food security.

Overall, the WTO's initiatives and policies supporting sustainable development demonstrate its commitment to ensuring that trade contributes to the well-being of people and the planet. By integrating economic, social, and environmental considerations into its work, the WTO plays a vital role in promoting a more sustainable and inclusive global economy.

This chapter explores the various initiatives and policies undertaken by the WTO to support sustainable development. It aims to provide a comprehensive understanding of how the organization addresses environmental and social concerns within the framework of international trade. Journalists, educators, scholars, politicians, diplomats, economists, legislators, and the public will find this chapter valuable in gaining insights into the WTO's role in promoting sustainable development and the impact of its policies on various aspects such as labor rights, intellectual property rights, fair trade practices, and gender equality.

Challenges and Criticisms of the World Trade Organization's Approach to Sustainable Development

The World Trade Organization (WTO) plays a crucial role in promoting sustainable development through its policies and agreements. However, its approach has faced significant challenges and criticisms from various stakeholders. This subchapter aims to explore these concerns and shed light on the potential drawbacks of the WTO's approach to sustainable development.

One of the main criticisms is that the WTO's focus on trade liberalization and market access often takes precedence over environmental and social considerations. Critics argue that the organization's primary objective of promoting free trade can undermine efforts to achieve sustainable development goals. They argue that trade liberalization can lead to increased resource exploitation, environmental degradation, and social inequalities, particularly in developing countries.

Another challenge is the lack of inclusivity in decision-making processes within the WTO. Developing countries often feel marginalized and voiceless in negotiations, making it difficult for their sustainable development concerns to be adequately addressed. This power imbalance raises questions about the fairness and effectiveness of the WTO's approach in promoting sustainable development.

Moreover, critics argue that the WTO's dispute settlement mechanism often prioritizes trade interests over environmental and social concerns. This can limit the ability of countries to enforce measures aimed at protecting the environment or promoting sustainable practices. Additionally, the WTO's intellectual property rights and patent protection regime has been criticized for impeding the transfer of environmentally-friendly technologies to developing countries.

Furthermore, the WTO's impact on agricultural subsidies and food security has drawn significant criticism. The organization's rules on agricultural trade have been accused of favoring developed countries, leading to unfair competition and undermining the livelihoods of small-scale farmers in developing countries. This, in turn, can have adverse effects on food security and sustainable agricultural practices.

Lastly, the lack of attention to gender equality in international trade is another concern. Critics argue that the WTO's policies and agreements fail to address gender disparities and may even exacerbate them. This oversight hampers efforts to achieve gender equality and sustainable development simultaneously.

In conclusion, while the WTO has made efforts to incorporate sustainable development into its agenda, there are several challenges and criticisms that need to be addressed. The organization must strike a better balance between trade liberalization and environmental/social concerns, ensure inclusivity in decision-making processes, and consider the impact of its policies on various stakeholders, particularly in developing countries. By addressing these concerns, the WTO can enhance its role in promoting sustainable development and contribute to a more equitable and environmentally-friendly global trading system.

Success Stories of Sustainable Development Promoted by the World Trade Organization

The World Trade Organization (WTO) plays a crucial role in promoting sustainable development across the globe. Through its various initiatives and agreements, the WTO has successfully contributed to the integration of economic, social, and environmental goals. This subchapter highlights some success stories of sustainable development promoted by the WTO, demonstrating its positive impact on the global economy and the well-being of nations.

One notable success story is the reduction of trade barriers for environmentally friendly goods and services. The WTO's Environmental Goods Agreement (EGA) aims to eliminate tariffs on a wide range of products that contribute to environmental protection. By facilitating the trade of these goods, the WTO encourages the adoption of sustainable technologies and practices, promoting a greener and more sustainable economy.

Another success story is the WTO's involvement in promoting renewable energy. The WTO has worked towards eliminating trade barriers and discriminatory practices that hinder the growth of renewable energy industries. Through its agreements, the WTO ensures a level playing field for renewable energy producers, enabling them to compete fairly in the global market. This has led to the expansion of renewable energy sectors in several countries, reducing dependence on fossil fuels and mitigating climate change.

The WTO has also played a crucial role in promoting sustainable agriculture. Through its Agreement on Agriculture, the WTO encourages the adoption of sustainable farming practices, such as organic farming and agroecology. By promoting fair and transparent agricultural trade rules, the WTO supports small-scale farmers in developing countries, enabling them to access global markets and improve their livelihoods sustainably.

Furthermore, the WTO's Trade Facilitation Agreement (TFA) has significantly contributed to sustainable development by simplifying and harmonizing customs procedures. This has reduced trade costs and enhanced the efficiency of cross-border trade, benefiting both developed and developing countries. By facilitating trade, the TFA promotes economic growth and poverty reduction, while also encouraging sustainable production and consumption patterns.

These success stories demonstrate the WTO's commitment to sustainable development. By promoting trade that is economically, socially, and environmentally sustainable, the WTO contributes to a more inclusive and prosperous global economy. However, it is essential to acknowledge that challenges and areas for improvement remain. The WTO must continue to address issues such as the impact of trade on labor rights, intellectual property rights, and gender equality, to ensure that sustainable development remains at the core of its agenda.

In conclusion, the success stories of sustainable development promoted by the WTO highlight the organization's positive impact on the global economy and the well-being of nations. Through initiatives such as the EGA, renewable energy promotion, sustainable agriculture, and trade facilitation, the WTO fosters a more sustainable and inclusive world. As the WTO continues to evolve and address emerging challenges, it remains an essential institution in advancing sustainable development goals globally.

Chapter 8: The World Trade Organization's Influence on Intellectual Property Rights and Patent Protection

Intellectual Property Rights and their Importance in Global Trade

In today's interconnected and globalized world, intellectual property rights (IPRs) play a crucial role in shaping international trade. Defined as the legal rights granted to individuals or organizations for their inventions, creative works, and trade secrets, IPRs are essential for promoting innovation, creativity, and economic growth. This subchapter will delve into the significance of intellectual property rights in the context of global trade, examining their impact on various stakeholders, including developing countries, consumers, and businesses.

First and foremost, intellectual property rights provide incentives for innovation and creativity. By granting exclusive rights to the creators and inventors, IPRs ensure that they can reap the benefits of their hard work and investments. This fosters a conducive environment for research and development, as individuals and companies are motivated to invest in new ideas, technologies, and artistic creations. Consequently, IPRs contribute to the advancement of society by driving innovation and technological progress.

Moreover, intellectual property rights are crucial in facilitating international trade. In a globalized economy, the exchange of goods, services, and ideas across borders is a common phenomenon. IPRs protect the rights of creators and innovators, ensuring that their products are not unlawfully copied or imitated. This, in turn, promotes fair competition and encourages investment in high-quality products and services. Without effective IPRs, businesses would be hesitant to engage in international trade, fearing that their intellectual property could be easily exploited by competitors.

Developing countries, in particular, stand to benefit from strong intellectual property rights. By protecting indigenous knowledge, traditional cultural expressions, and genetic resources, IPRs enable these countries to preserve their cultural heritage and capitalize on their unique resources. Additionally, robust IPR regimes attract foreign direct investment, as businesses are more inclined to invest in countries where their intellectual property is safeguarded.

However, it is important to strike a balance between promoting innovation and ensuring access to essential goods and services. One of the challenges associated with IPRs is the potential for monopolies and high prices, particularly in sectors such as pharmaceuticals. Therefore, policymakers and international organizations, such as the World Trade Organization (WTO), must address these concerns and find ways to reconcile the interests of different stakeholders.

In conclusion, intellectual property rights are invaluable in global trade, promoting innovation, protecting creators, and fostering economic growth. They provide the legal framework necessary for individuals and businesses to thrive in a globalized economy. However, it is crucial to ensure that IPRs strike the right balance between incentivizing innovation and ensuring access to essential goods and services. The World Trade Organization and other international bodies have a vital role to play in shaping intellectual property rights regimes that are fair, inclusive, and sustainable.

The World Trade Organization's Agreement on Trade-Related Aspects of Intellectual Property Rights (TRIPS)

The World Trade Organization's Agreement on Trade-Related Aspects of Intellectual Property Rights (TRIPS) is a crucial component of the global trade framework. TRIPS, established in 1994, sets out minimum standards for intellectual property (IP) protection and enforcement, aiming to strike a balance between promoting innovation and ensuring access to essential goods and services.

TRIPS addresses various forms of intellectual property, including patents, trademarks, copyrights, and trade secrets. It mandates that member countries provide a minimum level of IP protection, ensuring that creators and inventors can benefit from their work while fostering innovation and technological advancement.

One of the key objectives of TRIPS is to encourage the transfer of technology to developing countries. It recognizes the importance of technology in economic development and allows developing countries certain flexibilities to promote access to affordable medicines, educational materials, and agricultural technologies. These flexibilities include compulsory licensing, which enables governments to authorize the production of patented products without the consent of the patent holder in certain circumstances, such as public health emergencies.

However, TRIPS has faced criticism for potentially impeding access to essential medicines in developing countries. Critics argue that stringent patent protection can lead to high drug prices, making life-saving treatments inaccessible for many. Advocacy groups and civil society organizations have called for reforms to ensure that intellectual property rights do not hinder access to affordable healthcare.

Additionally, TRIPS has been a subject of debate regarding its impact on indigenous knowledge and traditional cultural expressions. Critics argue that the agreement fails to adequately protect traditional knowledge and may enable the misappropriation of indigenous resources and traditional practices.

Nevertheless, TRIPS has played a significant role in harmonizing international intellectual property standards and providing a framework for resolving disputes related to IP rights. The dispute settlement mechanism of the World Trade Organization has been utilized to address various IP-related issues, ensuring that member countries adhere to their obligations under the TRIPS agreement.

In conclusion, the World Trade Organization's Agreement on Trade-Related Aspects of Intellectual Property Rights (TRIPS) has been instrumental in establishing global standards for intellectual property protection and enforcement. While it has faced criticism for potentially hindering access to essential medicines and failing to adequately protect traditional knowledge, TRIPS has also provided a platform for resolving disputes and promoting innovation. As the world continues to grapple with the challenges of globalization, TRIPS and its implications for intellectual property rights will remain a critical topic of discussion for journalists, educators, scholars, politicians, diplomats, economists, legislators, and the general public.

Debates and Controversies Surrounding Intellectual Property Rights within the World Trade Organization

Introduction:

The World Trade Organization (WTO) is a global institution tasked with regulating international trade and promoting economic cooperation among its member nations. Intellectual Property Rights (IPRs) have become a vital issue within the WTO, leading to intense debates and controversies. This subchapter explores the various perspectives, concerns, and discussions surrounding IPRs and their impact on global trade.

Balance between Innovation and Access to Essential Medicines:

One of the most significant debates within the WTO is the balance between protecting intellectual property rights and ensuring affordable access to essential medicines, particularly in developing countries. Critics argue that stringent patent protection can hinder access to life-saving drugs, while proponents assert that strong IPRs are necessary to incentivize innovation and maintain research and development funding.

Protection of Traditional Knowledge and Biodiversity:

Another contentious issue is the protection of traditional knowledge and biodiversity. Developing countries often argue that traditional knowledge and genetic resources have been exploited by developed nations without adequate compensation or recognition. This has led to discussions on creating an equitable framework to protect traditional knowledge and biodiversity, while respecting IPRs.

Technology Transfer and Capacity Building:

Developing countries have long called for enhanced technology transfer and capacity-building measures to enable them to effectively utilize intellectual property for their own economic development. Critics contend that the existing framework favors developed countries and multinational corporations, limiting the ability of developing nations to benefit from their own intellectual creations.

Copyright and Digital Media:

With the rise of the digital era, copyright protection has become a contentious issue. The WTO faces debates over balancing the rights of content creators and consumers in the digital space. Questions surrounding fair use, digital piracy, and the role of internet service providers have sparked intense discussions on how to adapt copyright laws to the digital age.

Conclusion:

The debates and controversies surrounding intellectual property rights within the WTO reflect the complex and evolving nature of global trade. Finding a balance between protecting innovation, ensuring access to essential goods, and promoting equitable development remains a challenge. Addressing these concerns requires open dialogue, collaboration, and a deep understanding of the diverse perspectives and interests of all stakeholders involved. As the WTO continues to navigate these debates, it is crucial for journalists, educators, scholars, politicians, diplomats, economists, legislators, and the public to stay informed and engage in discussions that shape the future of intellectual property rights within the global trading system.

Case Studies Illustrating the Impact of the World Trade Organization on Intellectual Property Rights

In today's globalized world, intellectual property rights (IPRs) play a crucial role in fostering innovation, creativity, and economic growth. The World Trade Organization (WTO) has been at the forefront of shaping and enforcing international rules and regulations related to IPRs. This subchapter aims to provide a comprehensive understanding of the impact of the WTO on IPRs through a series of case studies.

One notable case study is the TRIPS Agreement (Trade-Related Aspects of Intellectual Property Rights), which came into effect in 1995. This agreement standardized IPR protection and enforcement mechanisms globally. As a result, countries like India faced challenges in implementing the agreement due to their domestic policies favoring affordable access to essential medicines. The case of India's patent law amendments, allowing for the production of generic versions of patented medicines, showcases how the WTO's influence on IPRs can clash with public health concerns.

Another case study is the dispute between the United States and China over intellectual property theft. The WTO has played a pivotal role in addressing this issue and fostering a more level playing field for international trade. The case highlights the challenges faced by developing countries in protecting their own intellectual property rights while also respecting the rights of foreign companies.

Furthermore, the WTO's involvement in the case of copyright infringement in the digital age is worth exploring. The rise of online piracy and illegal file-sharing platforms has posed significant challenges for copyright holders. Through the WTO's Agreement on Trade-Related Aspects of Intellectual Property Rights (TRIPS), member countries have worked together to establish stronger copyright protection measures and enforcement mechanisms.

These case studies illustrate the complex and evolving nature of the WTO's impact on IPRs. While the organization has made significant strides in harmonizing global standards, it also faces criticism for favoring the interests of developed countries over those of developing nations. As journalists, educators, scholars, politicians, diplomats, economists, legislators, and the public, understanding these case studies allows for a more informed assessment of the WTO's role in shaping IPRs and its potential implications on various stakeholders.

In conclusion, the impact of the WTO on intellectual property rights cannot be underestimated. Through analyzing case studies such as the TRIPS Agreement, the United States-China dispute, and copyright infringement in the digital age, we gain a comprehensive understanding of the challenges and opportunities that arise in the realm of IPRs. As we navigate the complexities of a globalized world, it is essential to continually evaluate the WTO's role in promoting fair and balanced intellectual property protection, fostering innovation, and promoting sustainable development.

Chapter 9: The World Trade Organization's Role in Promoting Fair Trade Practices

Fair Trade Principles and Objectives

Fair trade has become an increasingly important topic in the context of globalization and international trade. It seeks to address the imbalances and inequalities that can arise from the current trade system, particularly impacting developing countries and vulnerable communities. This subchapter explores the principles and objectives of fair trade and their significance within the framework of the World Trade Organization (WTO).

Fair trade encompasses a set of principles aimed at promoting equity, transparency, and sustainability in trade relations. It seeks to ensure that producers, especially those in developing countries, receive fair prices for their products and are provided with better trading conditions. These principles are based on the recognition that unfair trade practices, such as exploitative labor conditions, low wages, and environmental degradation, perpetuate poverty and hinder sustainable development.

The objectives of fair trade align closely with the goals of the WTO, which include promoting economic growth, development, and reducing poverty. Fair trade practices contribute to achieving these objectives by providing a platform for marginalized producers to access global markets on fair terms. By promoting ethical and sustainable production, fair trade contributes to the overall well-being of communities and protects the environment.

Within the WTO framework, fair trade principles and objectives are reflected in various agreements and initiatives. The WTO encourages member countries to consider the social and environmental impacts of their trade policies and to promote fair trade practices. It recognizes the importance of providing special and differential treatment to developing countries, acknowledging their specific needs and vulnerabilities.

Furthermore, fair trade is supported by a range of non-governmental organizations (NGOs) that play a crucial role in influencing the policies and practices of the WTO. These organizations advocate for fair trade principles, conduct research, and raise awareness among policymakers, educators, scholars, and the public. Their efforts contribute to shaping the discourse around fair trade within the WTO and promoting its integration into international trade agreements.

In conclusion, fair trade principles and objectives are essential in addressing the challenges posed by globalization and ensuring a more equitable and sustainable trading system. The WTO recognizes the significance of fair trade practices and encourages member countries to adopt measures that promote fairness, transparency, and sustainability. By embracing fair trade principles, the WTO can contribute to reducing poverty, promoting sustainable development, and fostering a more inclusive global economy.

The World Trade Organization's Efforts to Promote Fair Trade Practices

The World Trade Organization (WTO) has been at the forefront of promoting fair trade practices across the globe. As an international organization responsible for regulating and liberalizing international trade, the WTO plays a crucial role in ensuring that trade is conducted fairly and equitably.

One of the key ways in which the WTO promotes fair trade practices is through the enforcement of its rules and agreements. The WTO has developed a comprehensive set of rules that govern various aspects of international trade, such as tariffs, subsidies, and intellectual property rights. These rules provide a level playing field for all member countries, preventing unfair trade practices that could harm smaller or less developed nations.

Moreover, the WTO actively encourages its member countries to adopt fair trade practices through capacity-building programs and technical assistance. By providing training and support, the WTO helps countries, especially developing nations, to understand and implement the rules and agreements effectively. This promotes transparency and accountability in trade, ensuring that all countries have the knowledge and tools necessary to engage in fair and mutually beneficial trade.

Additionally, the WTO plays a crucial role in resolving trade disputes, further promoting fair trade practices. Through its dispute settlement mechanism, the WTO provides a forum for member countries to resolve conflicts and address unfair trade practices. This helps to maintain a stable and predictable trading environment, where countries can trust that their trade partners will abide by the rules and agreements set by the WTO.

Furthermore, the WTO recognizes the importance of sustainable development and promotes fair trade practices that take into account social, economic, and environmental considerations. The organization encourages its member countries to promote sustainable development through trade, ensuring that trade is not conducted at the expense of the environment or the well-being of local communities.

In conclusion, the WTO's efforts to promote fair trade practices are instrumental in creating a global trading system that is fair, transparent, and beneficial for all. Through its rules, dispute settlement mechanism, and capacity-building programs, the WTO ensures that trade is conducted in a manner that is equitable, sustainable, and respectful of the rights and needs of all nations. By promoting fair trade practices, the WTO contributes to a more inclusive and prosperous global economy.

Criticisms and Challenges of the World Trade Organization's Fair Trade Agenda

The World Trade Organization (WTO) has been at the forefront of promoting fair trade practices among its member nations. While its agenda aims to create a level playing field for all countries involved in international trade, there have been several criticisms and challenges that have emerged over time.

One of the main criticisms of the WTO's fair trade agenda is its failure to adequately address the concerns of developing countries. Many argue that the organization's rules and regulations disproportionately favor developed nations, leaving developing countries at a disadvantage. Critics argue that the WTO's focus on liberalization and deregulation often leads to the exploitation of developing countries' resources and labor, exacerbating inequalities between nations.

Another challenge faced by the WTO is the influence of non-governmental organizations (NGOs) in shaping its policies. While NGOs play an important role in advocating for social and environmental issues, their influence can sometimes hinder the efficiency and effectiveness of the WTO. Critics argue that the involvement of NGOs in the decision-making process can lead to delays and gridlock, making it difficult for the organization to fulfill its mandate.

Furthermore, the WTO's role in resolving trade disputes has also faced criticism. Some argue that the dispute settlement system is biased towards developed countries, as they tend to have more resources and legal expertise at their disposal. This perceived bias undermines the credibility and legitimacy of the WTO, raising questions about its ability to fairly resolve trade disputes.

The impact of globalization on the WTO has also posed challenges to its fair trade agenda. Globalization has led to increased interdependence among nations, making it difficult for the WTO to regulate and monitor trade practices effectively. The rapid growth of global supply chains and the rise of e-commerce have created new challenges for the organization, requiring it to adapt and evolve to keep up with the changing dynamics of international trade.

In conclusion, while the WTO's fair trade agenda aims to promote equitable and sustainable trade practices, it faces several criticisms and challenges. The organization must address the concerns of developing countries, navigate the influence of NGOs, enhance its dispute settlement system, and adapt to the complexities of globalization. Only by addressing these criticisms and challenges can the WTO effectively promote fair trade practices and fulfill its role in the global economy.

Examples of Successful Fair Trade Practices Supported by the World Trade Organization

The World Trade Organization (WTO) has played a crucial role in promoting fair trade practices around the world. Through its various agreements and initiatives, the organization has created an enabling environment for fair and equitable trade. Here are some examples of successful fair trade practices supported by the WTO:

1. The Bananas Dispute Resolution: One notable example is the long-standing bananas dispute between the European Union (EU) and several Latin American countries, including Ecuador, Colombia, and Costa Rica. The WTO facilitated negotiations and successfully resolved the dispute, ensuring fair access to the EU market for Latin American banana exporters.

2. The Ethiopian Coffee Trademark Case: In 2005, Ethiopia sought to trademark its specialty coffee names, such as Sidamo and Harar, to protect its unique products from misappropriation. With the support of the WTO, Ethiopia successfully registered its trademarks, allowing

farmers to earn higher prices for their coffee and preserving the country's cultural heritage.

3. The Access to Medicines Initiative: The WTO's Trade-Related Aspects of Intellectual Property Rights (TRIPS) agreement includes flexibilities that allow countries to protect public health and ensure access to affordable medicines. This has enabled countries like India to produce and export generic versions of essential medicines, improving access to life-saving drugs for millions of people in developing countries.

4. The Sustainable Fisheries Initiative: Recognizing the importance of sustainable fishing practices, the WTO has been actively involved in promoting sustainable fisheries. Through its negotiations, the organization has encouraged countries to adopt measures that prevent overfishing, protect marine ecosystems, and promote fair trade in fish and seafood products.

5. The Cotton Subsidies Case: The WTO has played a crucial role in addressing the issue of unfair subsidies in the cotton sector, which has disproportionately affected African cotton producers. Through negotiations and dispute settlement mechanisms, the WTO has worked towards reducing and eliminating subsidies, leveling the playing field for cotton farmers in developing countries.

These examples highlight the WTO's commitment to promoting fair trade practices across various sectors. By providing a platform for negotiations, facilitating dispute resolution, and ensuring the enforcement of trade rules, the organization has contributed to a more equitable global trading system. However, challenges remain, and continued efforts are needed to address the complex issues at the intersection of trade, development, and sustainability. The WTO must continue to evolve and adapt to the changing dynamics of globalization to foster fair trade practices that benefit all stakeholders involved.

Chapter 10: The World Trade Organization's Impact on Agricultural Subsidies and Food Security

The Relationship between Agricultural Subsidies, Trade, and Food Security

In recent years, the relationship between agricultural subsidies, trade, and food security has become a critical issue in global discussions. As the world population continues to grow, ensuring food security for all has become a top priority. However, the impact of agricultural subsidies and trade policies on food security has been a subject of debate.

Agricultural subsidies are financial incentives provided by governments to farmers to support their agricultural activities. These subsidies are intended to stabilize the agricultural sector, protect domestic farmers, and ensure food self-sufficiency. However, the implementation of these subsidies has raised concerns about their impact on trade and food security.

One of the main criticisms of agricultural subsidies is that they distort trade and create an uneven playing field for farmers in developing countries. Developed countries, with their substantial subsidies, can produce and export agricultural products at a lower cost, undermining the competitiveness of farmers in developing countries. This can lead to a decline in local agricultural production and an increased reliance on imported food, which can negatively impact food security.

Furthermore, agricultural subsidies can also have environmental consequences. Subsidies often encourage the overuse of water, fertilizers, and pesticides, leading to soil degradation, water pollution, and biodiversity loss. These environmental impacts can further undermine long-term food security.

To address these issues, the World Trade Organization (WTO) plays a crucial role in regulating agricultural subsidies and trade. The WTO's Agreement on Agriculture aims to establish fair and market-oriented agricultural trade by reducing trade-distorting subsidies and ensuring that domestic support does not undermine the food security of importing countries.

However, the effectiveness of the WTO's regulations on agricultural subsidies has been a subject of debate. Developing countries argue that developed countries should make significant reductions in their subsidies to level the playing field and promote fair trade practices. Some argue that the WTO's regulations do not go far enough in addressing the negative impacts of agricultural subsidies on food security and the environment.

To achieve food security and promote sustainable agriculture, a comprehensive approach is needed. This includes a combination of measures such as targeted support for small-scale farmers, investment in rural infrastructure, research and development for sustainable farming practices, and the promotion of regional trade agreements that take into account the specific needs and vulnerabilities of developing countries.

In conclusion, the relationship between agricultural subsidies, trade, and food security is complex and multifaceted. While agricultural subsidies can play a role in ensuring food self-sufficiency and stabilizing the agricultural sector, their implementation needs to be carefully managed to avoid negative impacts on trade and food security. The WTO's regulations on agricultural subsidies provide a framework for addressing these challenges, but further efforts are needed to promote fair trade practices and sustainable agriculture for the benefit of all nations.

The World Trade Organization's Policies and Agreements on Agricultural Subsidies

Introduction:

Agricultural subsidies have been a contentious issue in the global trade arena, with debates revolving around their impact on food security, trade distortions, and the interests of developing countries. The World Trade Organization (WTO) has played a crucial role in shaping policies and agreements regarding agricultural subsidies. This subchapter delves into the WTO's policies and agreements on agricultural subsidies, exploring the complexities and implications for various stakeholders.

Overview of the WTO's Approach:

The WTO's Agreement on Agriculture (AoA) is the primary framework governing agricultural subsidies. The AoA aims to promote fair competition, minimize trade distortions, and ensure food security. It classifies subsidies into three categories: domestic support, export subsidies, and market access barriers.

Domestic Support:

The WTO's policies on domestic support aim to strike a balance between supporting farmers and preventing unfair trade practices. The AoA sets limits on the overall level of support provided by member countries, establishing criteria such as the Aggregate Measurement of Support (AMS). Developing countries have more flexibility in their domestic support, recognizing their need for agricultural development.

Export Subsidies:

The WTO has made significant strides in reducing export subsidies through the Agreement on Agriculture. Developed countries committed to phasing out export subsidies, while developing countries were granted longer implementation periods. This approach aims to level the playing field and address concerns about unfair competition.

Implications for Food Security:

The WTO acknowledges the importance of food security and allows countries to take measures to safeguard their essential food stocks. However, such measures must be transparent, temporary, and not distort trade. The debate surrounding food security and agricultural subsidies remains contentious, with differing perspectives on how best to achieve both objectives.

Developing Countries' Interests:

The WTO recognizes the unique challenges faced by developing countries and strives to accommodate their concerns. Special and differential treatment provisions allow developing countries to implement policies that support their agricultural sectors. However, critics argue that more needs to be done to level the playing field and address the power imbalances between developed and developing countries.

Conclusion:

The WTO's policies and agreements on agricultural subsidies reflect the complex nature of global trade and the diverse interests of member countries. Balancing the need for fair competition, food security, and development remains a significant challenge. As debates continue, it is essential for journalists, educators, scholars, politicians, diplomats, economists, legislators, and the public to understand the implications of the WTO's policies and agreements on agricultural subsidies for various stakeholders. By engaging in informed discussions, stakeholders can contribute to shaping fair and sustainable global trade practices.

Criticisms and Controversies Surrounding the World Trade Organization's Approach to Agricultural Subsidies

Agricultural subsidies have been a subject of intense debate within the World Trade Organization (WTO) and among its member countries. This subchapter explores the criticisms and controversies surrounding the WTO's approach to agricultural subsidies, shedding light on the implications for global trade, food security, and developing nations.

One of the key criticisms leveled against the WTO's approach is the impact of agricultural subsidies on fair competition. Critics argue that the subsidies provided by developed countries to their farmers create an uneven playing field, making it difficult for farmers from developing nations to compete in the global market. This, in turn, perpetuates the cycle of poverty and dependency on food aid for many developing countries.

Moreover, the WTO's agricultural policies have faced criticism for their disregard of environmental sustainability. The heavy subsidies provided to farmers often incentivize overproduction, leading to environmental degradation, such as deforestation and excessive use of chemical fertilizers. These practices contribute to climate change and pose a threat to global food security in the long run.

Another contentious issue is the impact of agricultural subsidies on food security. Critics argue that the WTO's policies prioritize trade liberalization over ensuring access to affordable and nutritious food for all. By promoting the removal of trade barriers, the WTO inadvertently undermines the ability of developing countries to protect their domestic agriculture and ensure food self-sufficiency.

Additionally, concerns have been raised about the unequal distribution of subsidies among farmers. Small-scale farmers, particularly in developing nations, often receive disproportionately less support compared to their larger, industrialized counterparts. This exacerbates income inequalities and further marginalizes vulnerable communities.

Despite these criticisms, the WTO has taken steps to address some of these concerns. The Doha Development Agenda, launched in 2001, aimed to prioritize the needs of developing countries and address the imbalances within the agricultural subsidies regime. However, progress in these negotiations has been slow, with developed countries often reluctant to make significant concessions.

In conclusion, the WTO's approach to agricultural subsidies has faced significant criticisms and controversies. The impact on fair competition, environmental sustainability, food security, and the unequal distribution of subsidies are among the key concerns raised by various stakeholders. As the world grapples with the challenges of globalization and trade liberalization, it is crucial for policymakers, scholars, and the public to engage in a constructive dialogue to find viable solutions that promote equitable and sustainable agricultural practices within the WTO framework.

Case Studies Demonstrating the Effects of the World Trade Organization on Agricultural Subsidies and Food Security

Introduction:

The World Trade Organization (WTO) has played a significant role in shaping global trade policies, including agricultural subsidies and their impact on food security. This subchapter aims to present case studies that demonstrate the effects of the WTO on agricultural subsidies and food security, providing insights into the challenges and opportunities faced by different countries and regions.

Case Study 1: United States and European Union Agricultural Subsidies

The United States and the European Union (EU) have been at the center of debates surrounding agricultural subsidies. The WTO's Agreement on Agriculture aimed to reduce such subsidies to create a level playing field for all countries. This case study explores the impact of WTO regulations on the agricultural subsidies provided by these two major players, their effects on global food prices, and the resulting implications for food security.

Case Study 2: Developing Countries and Agricultural Subsidies

Developing countries often face challenges in competing with heavily subsidized agricultural products from developed nations. This case study examines the experiences of developing countries, such as Brazil and India, in navigating the WTO's regulations regarding agricultural subsidies. It sheds light on how these countries have utilized WTO provisions to protect their farmers, promote domestic food security, and pursue sustainable agricultural practices.

Case Study 3: Sub-Saharan Africa and Food Security

Sub-Saharan Africa, with its high dependence on agriculture, faces unique challenges in achieving food security. This case study delves into the impact of the WTO on agricultural subsidies in this region. It explores the potential conflicts arising from the liberalization of agricultural trade and the need to balance food security concerns. Additionally, it highlights successful initiatives and policy approaches adopted by certain African countries to address food security concerns while complying with WTO regulations.

Case Study 4: Sustainable Agriculture and Trade

The WTO plays a crucial role in promoting sustainable agricultural practices globally. This case study examines the efforts made by the WTO to incorporate environmental considerations, such as the reduction of chemical use and the protection of biodiversity, into trade policies. It showcases examples of countries that have successfully integrated sustainable agriculture practices with trade obligations, contributing to both food security and environmental sustainability.

Conclusion:

These case studies demonstrate the diverse effects of the WTO on agricultural subsidies and food security across different regions. They highlight the challenges faced by countries in balancing trade liberalization with the need to protect domestic farmers and ensure food security. By analyzing these case studies, journalists, educators, scholars, politicians, diplomats, economists, legislators, and the public can gain a comprehensive understanding of the complex interactions between the WTO, agricultural subsidies, and food security, which can inform policy debates and decision-making processes.

Chapter 11: The World Trade Organization's Role in Promoting Gender Equality in International Trade

Gender Equality and its Relevance to International Trade

In recent years, gender equality has emerged as a crucial issue in various domains, including international trade. The World Trade Organization (WTO) has recognized the importance of promoting gender equality in international trade and has taken steps to address this issue. This subchapter explores the relevance of gender equality to international trade and the role of the WTO in promoting gender equality.

Gender equality is not only a matter of human rights but also has significant economic implications. Studies have shown that gender equality can lead to increased productivity, economic growth, and poverty reduction. Therefore, ensuring gender equality in international trade is not only the right thing to do but also makes economic sense.

The WTO has recognized that gender equality is crucial for achieving its objectives of promoting economic growth and development through international trade. The organization has acknowledged that gender inequalities can limit the participation of women in trade and hinder economic progress. Therefore, it has taken steps to integrate gender considerations into its policies and activities.

One of the ways in which the WTO promotes gender equality is by encouraging its member countries to eliminate discriminatory trade practices that affect women. This includes addressing barriers that impede women's participation in international trade, such as gender-based violence, discriminatory laws, and regulations, and unequal access to resources and opportunities.

Furthermore, the WTO has also recognized the importance of collecting gender-disaggregated data on trade and economic indicators. This data can help identify gender-based disparities in trade and inform policy interventions to promote gender equality. By incorporating gender-specific data, policymakers can design targeted interventions to address gender inequalities in various sectors, such as agriculture, manufacturing, and services.

In addition to its internal efforts, the WTO also collaborates with other international organizations, non-governmental organizations, and civil society to promote gender equality in international trade. These collaborations involve sharing best practices, conducting research, and organizing capacity-building programs to enhance gender mainstreaming in trade policies and practices.

However, despite these efforts, challenges remain in promoting gender equality in international trade. Gender disparities persist in various aspects of trade, including access to finance, market opportunities, and participation in decision-making processes. Therefore, sustained efforts are required from all stakeholders to address these challenges and ensure that gender equality becomes an integral part of international trade.

In conclusion, gender equality is not only a matter of justice but also has significant implications for international trade and economic development. The WTO plays a crucial role in promoting gender equality by addressing discriminatory trade practices, collecting gender-disaggregated data, and collaborating with other stakeholders. However, more needs to be done to overcome the challenges and ensure that women can fully participate and benefit from international trade. By promoting gender equality in international trade, we can create a more inclusive and sustainable global economy.

The World Trade Organization's Initiatives to Promote Gender Equality

In recent years, the issue of gender equality has gained significant attention worldwide. As societies strive for progress and equality, it becomes imperative to ensure that international trade policies and practices are inclusive and promote gender equality. The World Trade Organization (WTO) recognizes this importance and has taken several initiatives to address gender disparities in international trade.

One of the key initiatives undertaken by the WTO is the establishment of the Women and Trade Program. Launched in 2017, this program aims to enhance the participation of women in international trade by addressing the specific challenges they face. Through research, capacity-building workshops, and policy dialogues, the program seeks to create an enabling environment for women entrepreneurs and traders to thrive.

Additionally, the WTO has integrated gender perspectives into its analytical work and research. By incorporating gender analysis into its reports and studies, the organization strives to better understand the impact of trade policies on women and identify areas where gender-responsive measures can be implemented.

Furthermore, the WTO promotes gender equality through its capacity-building initiatives. Through technical assistance and training programs, the organization helps developing countries enhance their understanding of gender issues in trade and develop strategies to mainstream gender equality in their national trade policies.

The WTO also engages in partnerships and collaborations with other organizations working towards gender equality. By collaborating with entities such as the International Trade Centre and the United Nations, the WTO leverages its expertise to support joint initiatives that promote women's economic empowerment and gender equality in trade.

However, it is important to acknowledge that challenges remain in advancing gender equality within the WTO. Critics argue that the organization's decision-making processes lack gender parity, and there is a need for greater representation of women in key positions. Addressing these concerns and ensuring gender equality within the organization itself is crucial to effectively promoting gender equality in international trade.

In conclusion, the WTO recognizes the significance of gender equality in international trade and has taken commendable initiatives to address this issue. Through its Women and Trade Program, integration of gender perspectives into research, capacity-building efforts, and collaborations with partner organizations, the WTO is striving to create a more inclusive and equitable trading system. Nonetheless, continuous efforts are required to overcome challenges and ensure that gender equality remains a priority within the organization and in the wider context of international trade.

Challenges and Limitations of the World Trade Organization's Efforts in Advancing Gender Equality

Introduction:

As the global economy becomes increasingly interconnected, achieving gender equality in international trade has emerged as a crucial goal. The World Trade Organization (WTO) has recognized this and has made efforts to promote gender equality within its framework. However, several challenges and limitations impede the organization's progress in this area.

1. Lack of gender-specific data:

One of the primary challenges faced by the WTO in advancing gender equality is the scarcity of gender-specific data. Without comprehensive and disaggregated data, it becomes difficult to identify and address gender disparities in international trade. Collecting gender-disaggregated data should be a priority for the WTO, as it would enable evidence-based policymaking and targeted interventions.

2. Limited representation and participation:

Although the WTO strives to be inclusive, women remain underrepresented in key decision-making positions within the organization. This lack of representation hampers the development of gender-sensitive policies and initiatives. To address this limitation, the WTO should actively promote gender-balanced representation in its leadership and committees.

3. Insufficient mainstreaming of gender in trade policies:

While the WTO has incorporated gender-related issues into some of its agreements, gender considerations remain largely on the periphery of trade negotiations and policies. There is a need for greater mainstreaming of gender in all aspects of the WTO's work, including trade rules, dispute settlement, and technical assistance programs.

4. Limited focus on informal and small-scale women traders:

The majority of women engaged in international trade operate in the informal sector or as small-scale traders. However, the WTO's efforts often overlook the specific challenges faced by these women, such as limited access to finance, market information, and trade facilitation services. The organization should develop targeted initiatives and capacity-building programs to support and empower these women traders.

5. Intersectionality and multiple layers of discrimination:

Gender equality cannot be achieved in isolation from other forms of discrimination. The WTO needs to recognize the intersectionality of gender with other factors, such as race, ethnicity, class, and disability. This requires a more holistic approach to gender equality, which takes into account the multiple layers of discrimination faced by marginalized women.

Conclusion:

While the WTO has taken steps towards promoting gender equality in international trade, several challenges and limitations persist. Overcoming these hurdles will require a concerted effort from policymakers, civil society, and the international community. By addressing these challenges and working towards more inclusive trade policies, the WTO can play a pivotal role in advancing gender equality and ensuring that the benefits of globalization are shared by all.

Success Stories of Gender-Inclusive Trade Policies Supported by the World Trade Organization

In recent years, the World Trade Organization (WTO) has made significant strides in promoting gender equality in international trade. By implementing gender-inclusive trade policies, the organization has not only empowered women but also contributed to the overall economic development of nations. This subchapter highlights some success stories that showcase the positive impact of these policies.

One such success story can be seen in Rwanda. With the support of the WTO, the Rwandan government implemented policies to enhance women's participation in trade. As a result, the country experienced a remarkable increase in women-owned businesses and their contribution to the economy. These policies provided training and financial assistance to women entrepreneurs, enabling them to access international markets and expand their businesses. Today, Rwanda has become a shining example of how gender-inclusive trade policies can lead to economic growth and empowerment.

Another success story comes from Bangladesh, a country known for its vibrant garment industry. The WTO worked closely with the Bangladeshi government to ensure gender equality in this sector. By promoting safe working conditions, fair wages, and equal opportunities for women, the WTO helped improve the lives of thousands of female garment workers. This not only empowered women but also enhanced the industry's reputation and competitiveness in the global market.

Furthermore, the WTO has played a crucial role in promoting gender equality in agriculture, a sector that employs a significant number of women worldwide. Through its programs, the organization has supported initiatives aimed at providing women farmers with access to training, resources, and markets. These efforts have led to increased productivity, income generation, and improved livelihoods for women in rural areas.

The success stories mentioned above are just a few examples of the positive impact of gender-inclusive trade policies supported by the WTO. By recognizing the importance of women's participation in international trade, the organization has helped bridge the gender gap and promote sustainable economic development. It is essential for policymakers, educators, scholars, and the public to acknowledge the significance of these success stories and advocate for further integration of gender perspectives in trade policies.

In conclusion, the WTO's commitment to promoting gender equality in international trade has yielded several success stories. Through its support for gender-inclusive trade policies, the organization has empowered women, enhanced economic growth, and fostered sustainable development. These success stories serve as inspiration for policymakers, economists, and scholars to continue advocating for gender equality in all aspects of global trade.